▣ DESIGN IDEAS FOR SMALL SPACES

Living Rooms & Home Offices

First published in the United States of America by:
Rockport Publishers, Inc.
146 Granite Street
Rockport, Massachusetts 01966-1299
Telephone: (508) 546-9590
Fax: (508) 546-7141

ISBN 1-56496-304-7

10 9 8 7 6 5 4 3 2 1

Layout: Sara Day Graphic Design
Cover Credit: See page 18

Printed by Welpac, Singapore.

▣ DESIGN IDEAS FOR SMALL SPACES

Living Rooms & Home Offices

Norman Smith

ROCKPORT
PUBLISHERS

Rockport Publishers
Rockport, Massachusetts

INTRODUCTION

Small space design is about making a lot out of a little. As prices for materials, labor and real estate continue to increase, our built environments have had to work harder, becoming more efficient and accommodating more activities in less space.

A small space can take many forms. It can be the tiniest possible office space with a minuscule work surface and tightly organized storage areas, or a medium-size room that is used as both an entertaining area and a study space. It might be a niche-like living room carved from the dining room, or a corner office/work space that reclaims valuable and unused floor space. It might be a loft that provides the additional floor area for a study, or custom cabinets that help divide the living room from the adjacent dining space.

A narrow but open rowhouse that relies on exposed structure, rather than standard walls, to suggest living areas is a good example of thoughtful small space design. Changes in ceiling height or color can create the impression of different areas—all without physically dividing the space. By the same token, imaginative and even daring uses of color, materials and surfaces can fool the eye into believing a space is larger than its true size.

The purpose of this book is to explore small space design by illustrating the many individual concepts and approaches of designers and architects confronted with the problems of small spaces. The living rooms and offices in these pages employ a variety of design tools or 'devices'. As you will see, while these devices appear again and again, their final effect changes according to the designer's choices, the use of the space, and the many other factors that go into a finished design.

No matter what the specific situation, a small space is never impossible to improve. Whether the design is professionally built or handled by a skilled homeowner, every small space can be made to appear larger and more attractive in ways that compensate for the shortcomings of its size.

DESIGN, AESTHETICS, AND STYLE

Photographer: Walter Smalling

A well-built design project must be detailed and constructed properly.

Creating a good design plan is a lot like sculpting a figure or painting a picture. Then, that thought is translated from the mind to reality in the same way that a sculptor begins with a block of stone or a painter moves to the canvas. Finally, the initial concept is refined using the tools of each person's trade. For a sculptor, a hammer and chisels bring the idea to light, while for the painter, brushes and pigments suffice. For the designer, the essential concept is first tempered by the need to satisfy three basic qualities. Paraphrasing an ancient architectural theorist, all designs must be well-built and useable while incorporating a strong measure of delight.

Each of these basics is related to all the others so that when artfully conceived, the whole is a wonderful sum of these parts. The loss of any one of these qualities or an imbalance among them can make a design lackluster and unusable.

The design starts with an essential concept much like a thought or a wish. In small space designs, this care is manifested by the artful detailing of portions of the design and by the efficient, imaginative, and conscientious use of materials. Sensitivity to the interior and exterior environment is an important part of building. Simultaneously, the manipulation of a room's proportions must come into play for both aesthetic effect and ease in construction. The use of symmetry or, alternately, asymmetry in the structural layout affects the cost of a design and its feeling of openness.

Along with the sense of construction, the design must be useable and must satisfy basic functional requirements. In a small space, this can be as simple as increasing light and air and as complicated as integrating multiple uses in a tightly defined room. Again, a designer's sense of appropriate proportions must come into play to help shape the space effectively.

Just as proportions affect the feel of a room, the use of one or more focal points can create the appearance of spaciousness or alternately that of a cozy and enclosed retreat within the space. Spatial and depth perception can be manipulated to visually transform a small space. For instance, a wall can be angled to counteract the natural shortening of perspective, making a room seem larger or longer, while still accommodating required traffic patterns through the space. The use of symmetry to balance competing elements can lend an air of quiet repose to a small room while providing for an efficient use of the space. In a different situation, an asymmetrical layout might help counter unequal uses and impart a feeling of dynamic excitement to an otherwise plain room. Continuity and discontinuity are also often associated with small space design. Making a surface discontinuous reinforces a sense of separation; on the other hand, a continuous patch of unbroken floor can be used to tie together several adjacent small spaces so that each appears a part of the others.

Delight is the third part of the essential triumvirate but it is of a piece with all the rest. Delight is often confused with aesthetics and style. However, aesthetics is really just the pursuit and appreciation of beauty in its many forms. Various styles are, and have become over time, the accepted manifestation of a current standard of beauty. However, the phrase 'aesthetics and style' is often used as though they have a life of their own and are merely a window dressing that can be applied to any room, almost like throwing on a change of clothes. Nothing could be further from the truth.

From a designer's standpoint the overall atmosphere of a space, or its aesthetic, is not simply a question of overlaying a style. Rather, it is dictated by the interaction of all three essential elements. These requirements are then filtered through the designer's mind and mixed with the variables of budget and other requirements to produce a final aesthetic that is appropriate for each particular situation.

Finally, the design is further refined and made concrete with the tools or devices of the designers trade to produce a final product. These devices are part and parcel of every small space design and, in different ways, will always reflect the three essential qualities and their related concepts.

Photographer: Walter Smalling

While it is possible to redo rooms in different period styles to pleasurable effect, the best small space designs don't start with a style but rather with the designer's and owner's fundamental thoughts and needs.

BASIC CONCEPTS OF SMALL SPACE DESIGN

A design is shaped by the designer's knowledge of how these qualities are first realized. This occurs through the use of the designer's equivalent of canvas or stone, using several basic design concepts including:

SYMMETRY/ASYMMETRY refers to a plan configuration or to the three-dimensional treatment of surfaces and planes within a space. In an effort to resolve fundamental building and design problems, designers have begun experimenting with more extreme forms of asymmetry. It is frequently used in small space design for exactly this reason.

PROPORTION is essentially the relationship of parts to the whole both in two dimensions and in three. Certain proportional relationships are pleasing to the mind and eye while others can create a disharmonious appearance.

FOCUS/FOCAL POINTS can be one of the basic building blocks of any small space design. Creating a main focal point in a small space can minimize other unattractive but necessary intrusions in the space. A focal point can be many things; a painting on a wall, the wall itself, a superb cabinet, a view outside, or any number of other items.

SPATIAL/DEPTH PERCEPTION relates to the overall appearance of a space. A skillful designer can deliberately manipulate elements of the design to make the room feel larger or smaller, shorter or taller, narrower or wider, depending on the situation.

CONTINUITY/DISCONTINUITY applies to the nature of a surface or to the layout of a plan. Continuity usually melds or ties together disparate elements; discontinuity heightens differences to create an appealing tension.

As a design progresses, these qualities and concepts are combined in any number of ways to refine the initial thought.

HOW TO USE THIS BOOK

For the purposes of this book, eight different devices have been chosen to help explain the different approaches of the various small space designs and their respective designers.

While no design will employ every possible device and some will certainly employ more than just a few, it's still possible to look at small space design as a compendium of these tools and to imagine how these devices might be applied to other designs, including your own.

Plan Organization

Basic plan devices include:

a. A layout of one or more spaces that incorporates circulation or alternately, that reconfigures a space to remove circulation in order to make the space more useable.

b. An orientation of a room or space to the outdoors to make the interior space feel larger. Aligning openings or using similar or sympathetic materials can help blend an interior space with an exterior space such as a patio or enclosed courtyard.

c. A physical connection or adjacency that opens up one or more areas to another.

Structure

Although structure may seem like just the utilitarian bones that help hold up roofs and floors, when expertly revealed and arranged, the structure defines space and suggests connections in very subtle ways.

Many designers will use structural necessities, such as bearing posts and beams, to create a delicate layering of line and shadow within a small space. This overlay can help define specific areas without the need for full-height walls, while still producing an overall feeling of openness.

Surfaces

Modulation of wall, ceiling, and floor surfaces can produce rich and varied textures that enliven even the smallest room. Surface variations can also be employed to affect how light fills the room. For instance, a mottled or highly textured surface diffuses light; while a polished or lacquered plane reflects it. Surface treatments range from basic wallpaper and paint to such esoteric materials as stainless steel, custom paint finishes, and special woods.

Color

Like surfaces, use of color can often make or break a design. In a small space, color can be used to highlight or de-emphasize a particular surface or object. Well chosen colors can be used to tie several small rooms together, or alternately, to subtly differentiate them. Color can be used to make surfaces recede or to draw them closer to the eye. Natural and artificial lighting greatly contributes to the perceived size of a room. Depending on the intention, a murky chiaroscuro or a bright, almost stark appearance can be used to open up a space or create a focus within a room.

Natural light can be introduced unaltered via windows and skylights or it can be filtered and modified through deep recesses, window treatments or other means. Lighting fixtures are currently available in an almost bewildering array of types and designs. Like natural light, artificial lighting can be used indirectly to merely suggest a warm glow or at the other extreme, the lighting fixture itself can be made a bright and dazzling centerpiece to the room.	**Lighting**
Attention to details such as trim, connections, and hardware is important in all designs, but in a small space the importance of detail cannot be overlooked. Well-crafted details can suggest a richness that belies a small project budget. At the same time, details can introduce a perceptual scale change that camouflages the true dimensions of a small space.	**Trim and Detail**
Connecting inside and outside spaces is a time-honored device that is particularly appropriate to small space design. By sharing or borrowing space from the outside, almost any room can be made to feel larger and more gracious. The connection may be as simple as a lushly planted garden casually placed outside a pair of glass doors or as complicated as the rigorous use of similar or sympathetic materials that continue from indoors to the outside.	**Inside and Outside**
Designers often employ built-in and carefully selected pieces of furniture to maintain and reinforce their aesthetic intent. In a small space, this aesthetic control is still important but furniture design and placement can, quite simply, save space—or at least use the space more efficiently. Striking material palettes in furniture can also be used to complement the background surfaces.	**Furniture**

Not all of these design devices are appropriate for every project; using every device in a small project would be like ordering every item from an a la carte menu; the meal would simply be too large, too rich, and lacking the focus of a single well executed entree. In much the same way, most designers go through an editing process to try to achieve a simplicity and clarity of design. As you will see, each project illustrated in this book utilizes one or more of these design devices to make a small space useable and, at the same time, a delight to use.

Living Rooms

Traditionally, the living room has been devoted to formal uses such as entertaining guests. At the same time, the activities that are a day to day part of family life often need to be accommodated in the same space. Modern living rooms are therefore faced with the unenviable job of satisfying both formal and informal needs in a constantly shrinking footprint.

One solution is to use various techniques to make a small and basically informal space appear grander and more formal than it might be otherwise. Another option is the combined use of space that sets aside various discrete entertaining and play areas within the larger whole.

When designing or considering a living space, it's important to keep in mind what the space will actually be used for. Many times, the living area is combined with eating spaces and will require some separation between the two. Often in a small space design, the living area will also double as or be adjacent to an entry; environmental concerns as well as the need for privacy will then come into play.

The overall atmosphere of the space is also very important. Designs for small living spaces must take into account whether the space is formal or informal, open to the outside or closed off within other areas, and whether the space will have one purpose or many. As with small kitchens, equipment integral to the room's function — such as televisions and stereos — must also be accommodated.

The basic design approach to small living rooms is to mold the existing space: Surfaces and colors will help to differentiate adjacent areas, while the use of trim and thoughtful massing can be used to suggest space where none actually exists.

SMALL LIVING ROOMS

Photographer: Undine Prohl

OPEN PLAN LIVING ROOM

A small house appears deceptively large through the imposition of a simple plan organization. Inside the house shell the new plan creates a single large living space. Adjacent spaces arranged around the living area remain visually separate, but share in the large space's grandeur.

The plan layout creates a recognizable central, circular area that recalls classically inspired designs.

Lighter value colors on the walls and columns of the living area are offset by darker hues on the adjacent walls.

Wall-washing light fixtures at the edge of the living area highlight the central space without harshness.

Built-in seating saves space at the living room's perimeter and allows room for several, carefully chosen furnishings in the center.

Photographer: Henry Bowles

BASEMENT FAMILY ROOM

In this narrow family room, a mixture of painted finishes and light wood, along with thoughtful lighting layout, creates a restrained and relaxed space that belies its below-ground origins. The room occupies only a small portion of the basement and accommodates television and audio visual equipment.

 Exposed-bearing columns are accommodated in the overall layout and help to differentiate the seating and circulation areas.

 Portions of the floor and built-in shelves share a common surface material palette which minimizes changes in plane and gives the room a pleasing but restrained appearance.

 Indirect ceiling lighting offers the illusion of daylight through a series of curved, coffer-like baffles.

 Small details, like the interweaving of shelving edges and the gypboard surface, provide a visual and tactile continuity that makes the space seem larger.

Photographer: Julia Heine

SPLIT-LEVEL LIVING ROOM

This combination entertaining area, work-space, and gallery began life as an unused and disconnected portion of a split-level home. The space was reclaimed by removing a wall to open the new area onto an adjacent stair hall.

Simple interior massing creates the feel of a tall space although one portion of the room is fairly low.

A suspended lighting grid accommodates gallery-type lighting as well as video viewing; a mixture of fluorescent colors draws the eye upward.

A free-standing 'architectural canopy' marks the entry from both gallery apse and stairwell.

Photographer: Alex Nitsch

Photographer: Peter Olson

A loft-like aesthetic is strengthened by the use of an apparently massive, exposed structure.

Wood framing and a dark stone floor contrast with the modern art in a balanced but provocative composition.

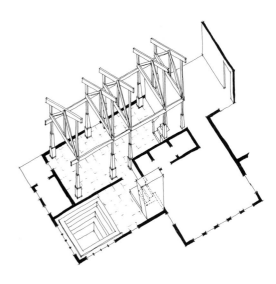

GALLERY LIVING ROOM ADDITION

This one-story addition provides both entertaining space and a gallery area for the owner's Modern art collection. A straight-forward plan layout and simple materials palette reinforce the living room's clear design concept.

17

MINIMALIST LIVING ROOMS

 A stucco-like surface finish on the cylindrical wall and the aperture window are the highlights and focal points of this scaled down room.

Photographer: Undine Prohl

Photographer: Douglas Hill

 The saturated color of a terra cotta fireplace wall exaggerates the scale of a standard fireplace in this modest living room.

Cathedral Living Room

Compact spatial and volumetric organization of the interior and exterior results in efficient, combined living and kitchen spaces within the cathedral-ceilinged portion of this small house.

Exposed collar ties high on the ceiling lend an air of shade and drama to the space.

Photographer: Robert Perron

Loft Living Rooms

Photographer: J.D.Peterson

Three interconnected landmark buildings were redeveloped to include 127 individual live/work lofts arranged around three interior courtyards. The buildings' existing structures were left in place along with a well-known clock tower to create an atmosphere that has been likened to a 'city quarter'

 In this compact unit, the bedroom loft within a loft is placed above the kitchen but left only partially enclosed; drapes provide privacy when desired.

 Various metal fabrications by local artists and crafts-people serve as a compelling counterpoint to the old building, and visually organize the common open space.

 Massive posts and beams contrast with the painted walls and delicate lighting fixtures.

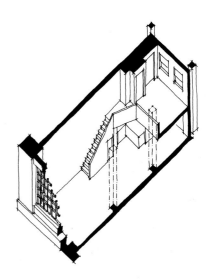

COLUMNED FAMILY ROOM

This basement family room provides seating areas around a fireplace and adjacent area to maximize the use of the entire space. The necessary steel columns are incorporated in the design and help to differentiate the two areas; they also provide a vertical counterpoint to the horizontal soffits and fairly low ceiling.

Lighting at the top of the columns makes these structural components a positive element in the low space.

A bank of wood and steel cabinetry contrasts with the subdued carpet color and painted gypboard surfaces.

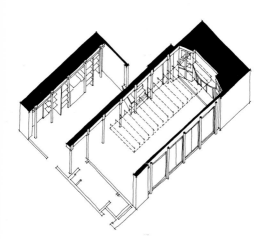

Photographer: Shorieh Talaat Design Associates

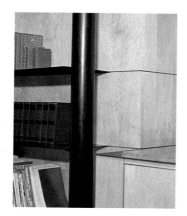

22

RENOVATED 1942 TOWNHOUSE LIVING ROOM

Removing a kitchen wall in this 1942 townhouse improved circulation throughout.

Instead of enclosing the new pathway in a hall, the architect kept the space open but defined it with a multi-colored, vinyl tile flooring.

Minimal but detailed railings render the stair an object within the narrow living area.

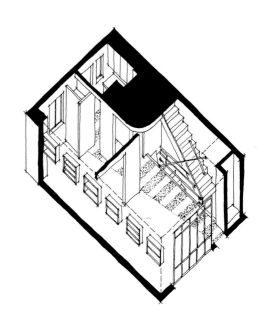

Photographer: Kendall Dorman

PANELED LIVING ROOM

Lushly paneled wall surfaces lend a textural richness to a diminutive living space.

Mirrored shelving units, and space opening into the next room helps suggest expansiveness beyond that of the living room itself.

Photographer: Andrew Bordwin

Photographer: Bruce Katz

SIMPLE PLAN LIVING ROOM

Application of simple wood trim on the walls creates a paneled effect that breaks up the wall plane without diminishing this small space.

The subtle use of color on the walls gives this small living room an intimate atmosphere, without making it seem cramped.

Home Offices

Until the beginning of this century, working at home was an accepted practice for many people. Often, shop proprietors lived above or beside their premises, tradespeople had shops attached to or near their homes, and doctors, lawyers, and other professionals practiced out of their homes. This gentle and environmentally sound practice has recently come back into favor. The advent of efficient telecommunications, changes in the demographics and duties of the work force, as well as the problems of commuting have conspired to make the home office a viable alternative for many workers.

For most home office users though, there is little excess space to devote to the office itself and so this space can sometimes be treated with less respect and design consideration than it deserves. On the other hand, a small space, as elsewhere in the house, can be used and enjoyed to full advantage when it is well designed.

The many prerequisites of the office include communications and equipment as well as privacy from living areas. All of these can be incorporated and balanced under the umbrella of a strong initial design concept and realized through the thoughtful use of design devices to create a work space or spaces that restore both the joy and dignity of work.

SMALL HOME OFFICES

Photographer: Woody Cady

Although it appears spacious, the studio is really just an enlarged landing at the top of the stairs.

REMODELED ATTIC OFFICE

An attic remodeling of this older home in a historic suburban neighborhood creates a small studio space at the top of the stair. A modest, new dormer with large central window and smaller flanking units brings in light and suggests a garret-like atmosphere.

CONVERTED GARAGE OFFICE

The design of this architect's office (located in a garage) fools the eye into believing the space is much larger than its small footprint. Varying wall surfaces and indirect lighting of the first floor from the rear stair suggest the possibility of much larger spaces beyond.

 On the lower level, a single cathedral-ceilinged space contains a circular stair and a small kitchenette as objects within the room.

 Varying the paint treatments on the wall helps break up space without physically dividing it, and makes it easy for clients in the office to see different options.

Photographer: Woody Cady

Photographer: Tim Street-Porter

Artist's Studio

This studio space for an artist and printer incorporates living and working areas within a small, carefully modulated envelope. Studio spaces are open to the kitchen and eating areas on the lower level, and to a tiny sleeping loft via the stair. Because the studio's location is screened by an existing house, views outward are carefully controlled to maintain an overall feeling of spaciousness.

 Work and living areas are left open to one another.

 Outside, a muted palette of earthy colors helps to blend the house with its small garden.

 Large, carriage-type doors provide accessibility and connection to the outside.

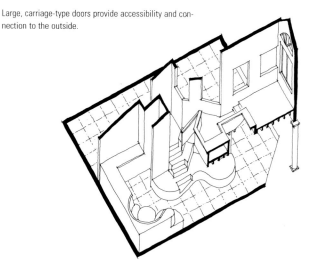

Photographer: Woody Cady

HOME OFFICE ADDITION

A narrow, bay-like addition along one side of the house creates a desk area for this home office remodeling. Work surfaces, files, and other storage are neatly incorporated within a shallow bumped-out space. Three large skylights in the sloping ceiling allow natural light to pour into the room.

Skylights and side windows provide illumination at the desks and also help to light the remainder of the room.

A neutral palette keeps the small space light.

33

MULTI-PURPOSE OFFICE

This combination living and home office space for architects makes the most of a small, and oddly shaped footprint. Height changes of several risers help differentiate work and living areas, while still allowing the entire area to be read by the eye as one large space. Inexpensive detailing of exposed structure and sliding doors adds a level of architectural elaboration to the simply finished space.

Photographer: Joseph Pro

 Small drafting work areas are placed on either side of the stair and look outward through a wall of windows.

 Beams painted red provide a counterpoint to the otherwise neutral palette.

 Use of wood trim and basic polycarbonate glazing creates a minimal but elegant door to the living area.

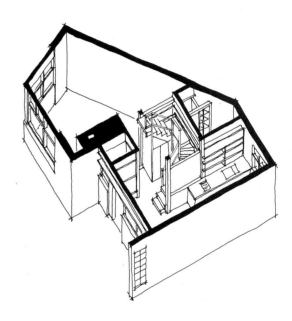

Photographer: Joseph Pro

35

LOFT OFFICE

 A post and beam structure within the house creates a combination study and occasional guest room.

 Large windows at the loft's floor level extend the perceived space.

Photographer: John Wiebenson

Photographer: Norman Smith

SHARED OFFICE/LIBRARY

Varying pastels on soffits and ceiling contrast with the adjacent hallway of books to clearly define the office area.

Concealed uplights balance the soffit-mounted downlights to softly illuminate and lift the cathedral ceiling.

A hallway becomes a book gallery using custom cherry, mahogany, and birch shelving units.

WINDOWED OFFICES

 An austere but sensuous vaulted ceiling has a wonderfully rough, tactile quality that shapes and distributes light from the window.

Photographer: Undine Prohl

 A hinged desktop creates a sun-filled work area and can be swung out of the way for door access.

Photographer: Andrew Bordwin

Photo: Cindy Linkins

SHARED STUDIO

A studio space shared by two artists is terminated at one end by a full height angled bay window. The bay uses 'Kalwall' a sandwich of translucent plastic in a rigid frame to control and modulate direct sunlight into a soft, general illumination.

 At night, the bay is lit from inside with a ceiling mounted spot.

 The lightly textured surfaces of the bay panels are an effective counterpoint to the clear-coated particle board floors.

TWO-STORY OFFICE

 Necessity becomes virtue by painting and detailing a support column for a bay-like space above.

 In a space that might have been only a standard stair, the architect creates a library and alternating-tread stair to a loft area above.

 The visually lightweight stair construction and open walkway above create a minimal intrusion in the small space.

Photographer: Undine Prohl

40

DIRECTORY OF ARCHITECTS

DIRECTORY OF CONTRACTORS

DIRECTORY OF PHOTOGRAPHE

Andrew Bordwin
70 A Greenwich Avenue #332
New York, NY 10011

Henry Bowles
933 Pico Boulevard
Santa Monica, CA 90905

Woody Cady
Woody Cady Photography
4512-A Avondale Street
Bethesda, Maryland 20814

Kendall Dormann
1739 Connecticut Avenue NW
Washington, DC 20009

Julia Heine
310 1/2 A Street NE
Washington, DC 20002

Douglas Hill
2324 Moreno Drive
Los Angeles, CA 90039

Bruce Katz
2700 Connecticut Avenue NW
Washington, DC 20008

Cindy Linkins
Shorieh Talaat Design Associates
15715 Kruhm Road
Burtonsville, MD 20866

Alex Nitsch
Swallow's Studio
422 Business Center
P.O. Box 839
Oaks, PA 19456

Peter Olson
211 North 13th Street
Philadelphia, PA 19107-1624

Undine Pröhl
1930 Ocean Avenue #302
Santa Monica, CA 90405

Walter Smalling
1541 Eighth Street NW
Washington, DC 20001

Norman Smith
3800 Military Road NW
Washington, DC 20015

Tim Street-Porter
2074 Watsonia Terrace
Los Angeles, CA 90068

Shorieh Talaat Design Associates
15715 Kruhm Road
Burtonsville, MD 20866

Christopher Vendetta
649 South Henderson Road
Apartment C 402
King of Prussia, PA 19406

John Wiebenson
Wiebenson & Dorman Architects
1739 Connecticut Avenue NW
Washington, DC 20009